LIGHT RELFECTIONS
By Tyrean Martinson

Published by Tyrean Martinson
Wings of Light Publishing
Copyright © 2014 Tyrean Martinson
ISBN: 978-0-9889933-3-4
Photography by Tyrean Martinson
Copyright © 2014 Tyrean Martinson

This book is dedicated to Jesus, My Savior, and to friends and family who have cheered every writing endeavor, long or short.

Contents

FOREWORD

I never set out to write poetry. I started poetry as a writing exercise to bring life to my prose. One day, in college, I perused the student newspaper and thought that some of my poetry might fit in the poetry section. I submitted three poems, and two were published within the week. It was a heady responsibility. I sent two more poems in, and had both published. Then, I waited more than a decade to try again. My poetry has found a home online in various places like *Figment*, *Bewildering Stories*, *Every Day Poets, Moon Drenched Fables* (no longer in existences) and *Haruah* (no longer in existence). Some of the poems in this collection have been previously published, and some are new to print of any kind. All of these poems were written between 2008 and the end of 2012. I included one short story, because, somehow, it seemed to fit with these light reflections.

Tyrean Martinson

MARCH SNOW HARE
(Previously published at Every Day Poets)

My beagle finds
A rabbit hole.
Alice, are you there?

White-etched ferns
and blackberries crowd
to hide the quivering hare.

Full flakes of whirling
March snow fall thick
on my tongue, my breath
hangs quiet in the air.

WEATHER'S ARGUMENT

Hail from March skies
turns to wonder-filled snow
then pitters into rain.

Sun breaks out to blaze
down on us, blessed warmth,
for a single hour.

Gray clouds gather again,
pour rain, fluff into cold snow
slushes on the street.

Rainbow moment 'til
dark disperses the argument
until tomorrow.

Tyrean Martinson

MARCH WRITING WEATHER

March writing has been
like the weather this year,
first warm, then cold, ever
changing with sun, wind, rain,
hail, snow, and sun again.
Frost on the ground for days,
then flowers bloom in bright sunlight.
Starting and stopping growth, never
content with a blank page.

GRANDPA'S APRIL FOOLS

Thirty years ago today
I watched a man die.
We were praying,
My family, the priest, and I

When I peeked through my eyelashes
At the walls, the calendar, the window sashes,
The sunshine outside, and finally,
The bed, and my grandpa's quiet face

His eyes were closed, at peace,
Then his raspy breathing seemed
To disappear, and his chest stilled.
His hand lay on the blanket

Where I could see his fingers
Fade from pinkish to bluish,
And I tugged my mother's arm.
She hushed me,

And I tugged again.
Finally, she listened,
The pastor finished his prayer,
And they knew what I knew.

My Grandpa was dead
on April Fool's day,
and I saw him take his last breath.
I think sometimes that he

Tyrean Martinson

would not like the fact
that I have never played
an April Fool's joke.
I should honor his memory.

Light Reflections

APRIL SECOND
(Previously published at Every Day Poets)

My aunt didn't believe us
when we told her
Grandpa died
on April Fool's day.

In her hatred,
she thought it was
some kind of sick joke,
no matter our tears.

On April second,
she finally knew.
She said, "Thank God
that d@#n b@%$@*d's dead."

I hated her for that,
but thirty years later
she breathes life with gasps.

I wish I could play at April Fool's
but never learned how
and
she never learned
to laugh.

Yet, that must be wrong,
 because once
 I heard her husky

Tyrean Martinson

laughter pour out like
rain after a drought.

I have to hold onto that,
not allow grief
to trick memory,
a fool's joke gone wrong,
a funeral song
at Easter.

Light Reflections

haiku - Daffodils

daffodils trumpet
their wide maned beauty, reaching
up from the green grass

Tyrean Martinson

haiku - lemonade

pulpy lemonade
tastes just as sweet on cloudy days
with a hint of sun

Light Reflections

haiku - breeze

The breeze dances with
branches budded with blossoms,
raindrops, and promise

Tyrean Martinson

haiku - forgiveness

Forgiveness unfolds like
the petals of a flower
in the bloom of spring.

RAIN DROP

Wet, dripping rain
falls from the rooftops,
plip plop, slop, drop.

Mud puddles grow
and if I could, I would
skip, hop, slip, and slop -

Wet, puddles filling
in my jean cuffs,
so they flip, flop, sop.

A good day for any rain drop.
Ker-plop.

Tyrean Martinson

RAIN AND RAINBOWS

A cloudy sunny day,
only in the Northwest
we see such weather.

A little bit of everything
all mixed together.
all the colors God created.
all the seasons in one day.

We have wind,
sun, hail, and rain.
Why complain?

We are a land
    of Rainbows

TULIP AND EVERLASTING

A tulip stands tall amongst
the flowers my mother calls everlasting.
Pink, rounded edges on a straight stem,
and purple tufts branching up and outwards,
show life, fleeting and forever,
precious in any form, for any season.
Reminding me to measure this world
against the length of eternity.
When the tulip dies, the everlasting will live.

Tyrean Martinson

FRUIT SALE CINQUAIN

(Previously published at Every Day Poets)

fruit sale
plump deceivers
beckon with bright skin
once bitten, pain puckers my lips
sour grapes

LEAVING DAY

Over-stuffed bags and scribbled lists
    Books, and passports,
A well-loved teddy bear
    A house standing open to the air.
Searching for that last thing, and saying goodbye
    We've made our reservations.
"Did we forget the kitchen sink, a toothbrush, our socks?"
    We'll know when we get to our destination.

Tyrean Martinson

ROAD TRIP

Water bottles and snacks
    Dog-eared books, and a candy wrapper,
The hum of tires on the road,
    Each city we pass is like a new chapter.
Listening, and looking,
    Letting the maps slip from our grip,
"Are we there yet?"
    All this makes for a good road trip.

NO VACANCY

Gritty eyes search
for a neon vacancy
but Moab is full
of travelers lured
by Arches and Canyons
vast   spaces
filled by cars on
endless highways.

Tyrean Martinson

HERE OR THERE
(Previously published at Every Day Poets)

Sunlight dances off water
drips from my scrub brush on
a white deck gleaming beneath
my feet, rocked gently by the
cul-lap-gurgle of Lake Union's waters.

I straighten with one hand on my
sweat-covered back aching
from scrubbing decks, sides, tops
of a fleet of yachts all in dock.

Boats line the blue horizon,
untouched except for a weekend
here or there, scrub brushes,
Canadian geese droppings, spiders
swinging in corners, waiting for prey.

On the weathered dock, a man asks
if I am working my way up for a life
of boat ownership. I laugh.
If I could,
I would buy that –

I squint into the sun and point
to a seaplane that comes to land -
a soft skimming water splash
that sends a rocking
wake against the docks.

Light Reflections

Flight, air, water, freedom
call like a Siren
with the buzz-melody of a floatplane,
but for now I bend back to my work,
swabbing the deck clean life's traces
waiting for that weekend here or there.

Tyrean Martinson

ECHOES
(Previously published online at Haruah)

Waves crashing, roaring
tumbling into foam that seeps
up the sandy shore.

Our feet sink lower
as the water rushes out
leaving our imprints

behind us like the
echo of our lives filled with
the love of Christ.

WHITE ROSE PETALS
(Previously published at Yahoo Associated Content)

White rose buds,
scorched and curled brown,
    bend
 to rain damp earth,
drinking life through quiet roots,
bowing with the heavy drops
of new hope.

Tyrean Martinson

MY MOTHER'S COMPOST

(Previously published at Every Day Poets, and caused a small discussion about composting. A relatively less known fact in composting: rats actually eat vegetables and fruit.)

My mother's compost churns
dead clippings, old leaves,
fruit peelings, and withered
lettuce, all moldering into rich,
black soil, home of insects, worms
and snails, visited by raccoons and
rats taking their share off the top.

Days , weeks, and months see the
heap grow, until the edges soften with
muddy seasons and sun, when weeds
dance around the edges, proclaiming
life abundant. My mother smoothes
the soil with care and plants anew,
in an overgrown Eden of green.

BUTTERFLY

I saw a wild fluttering butterfly
I saw it zigzagging in the blue sky

Flashing bright colors, it swooped and dipped down
Exploding orange, blue, white, it landed

On my outstretched hand where it flexed its wings
Inquisitively inviting my soul to sing

Tyrean Martinson

LIGHT REFLECTIONS

Light reflections
on the underside of
    scattered
clouds,
shimmering
the blue sky
gold.

HAPPINESS IS

Happiness is:
the blue sky with soft clouds,
the soft furry purring of a cat,
the prancing of a happy dog at play,
the laughter of daughters dancing,
the warmth of my husband's embrace.

Happiness is:
the joy of the Lord surpassing sadness,
the salty tang of the sea air by our home,
the light that shines in the darkness,
the multi-colors of stained glass,
the tapping of feet to inner music,
the sound of my husband's heartbeat.

Happiness is:
muddy feet and wet puddles to splash in,
abundant ripe blackberries picked among thorns,
the coolness of pool water on hot skin,
the smell of over-ripe apples picked by the birds,
the humming of bees busily sipping nectar,
my husband's voice, chuckling with a private joke.

Happiness is:
crisp, cold air on a bright blue day,
snow covered mountain peaks,
fresh powder on a groomed run,
my daughters' jumps off moguls,
the burn of my thighs on a black diamond run,

my husband's turning form, his stalls, his smile.

Happiness is:
budding trees by my porch,
croaking frogs along our drive,
birds who watch us with curious eyes,
the flight of a crane that stood still for a moment,
the arc of a Frisbee thrown between sisters,
the blue sky laughter of my husband's eyes.

TEMPTED TO WAKE YOU

In the half-light of morning
your face is softened by sleep,
your arms loosely curled
about your chest, and I reach
for you because I know how sweet
the sandy smoothness of your stubbled
cheek is to my fingers, and I long
to wake you with a kiss.

Instead I run my fingers
in your short silky curls, and
watch you breathe, taking in
the rest you need for the day ahead.
You stir, and I withdraw my hand, content,
knowing that you are my beloved,
a gift to me from God,
the perfect mate for my heart, and when you
wake I'll be here beside you.

Tyrean Martinson

WHEN WE ARE ONE

Speaking together in the church
vowing in our own words
we are one
Sleeping together amidst the covers
dreaming our own dreams
we are one
Laughing together over a joke
chuckling in our own voices
we are one
Weeping together over a loss
clinging to one another
we are one
Sitting together on the couch
reading our own books
we are one
Bickering together in the kitchen
teasing each other out of anger
we are one
Listening together to music in the car
thinking our own thoughts
we are one
Working together in the yard
using our own tools
we are one
Journeying together through life
drawing closer each day
we are one

POETRY'S TASTE

Poetry's taste is
sweet on the tongue, like a smile
or a lingering kiss.

Tyrean Martinson

BLANK PAGE

A blank page frightens
me, freezing my blood, leaving
emptiness within.

So I strike out with
my mind, and then finally
a single keystroke.

The page is no longer
blank, and the keystrokes flow like
living liquid, filling the page,

filling me with hope
and surety of purpose
with each conquered page.

AS THE LEAVES FALL

As the leaves fall golden,
rusty and pumpkin colored,
breezes send them skidding.
My dog leaps and pounces,
hoping for a squirrel chase.

He sniffs a giant curled maple,
snorts, and looks at me as if
I've hidden a squirrel in my pocket
and replaced it with the leaf.

Tyrean Martinson

SONNET OF LEAVES
(Previously published on my blog and the winner of a Shakespeare Sonnet blog fest)

Leaves flicker in winds, flames against blue sky
Reds, golds, oranges, all bright and living still
for a short time they dwell on branches high.
As the cold seeps in, bringing winter chill,
hard rains, darkening clouds like seasons' night,
they fall in drifts of crackling wonderful
sound for our passing, joyful delight
until trampled muddy and disgraceful
when we rake them together for compost,
laid near by roots of trees and over garden beds.
Nutrients for next year's colorful boast
sink down to rise up again overhead.
Each leaf a living miracle of life
showing promise in spite of fallen strife.

LET THE WILD RUMPUS BEGIN IN A LIBRARY
(Previously published on my Figment account)

Once upon a time in a basement library nook
I stumbled upon my first favorite book
Pulled into adventure as the pages unfurled
I found treasures greater than gold or pearls

In a book that took me sailing through night and day
I joined in the wild rumpus just long enough to say
a home with love and a supper waiting, nice and hot
was more important than being Queen or King on the spot.

My imagination took me swinging through trees,
and I could return home when I pleased.
I met wild characters and creatures from many lands
and had adventures in mountains, seas and sands.

Once upon a time in a basement library nook,
I fell in love with the soft pages of a book.
The pages turned, the adventures unfurled,
    and I held a treasure greater than gold or pearls

Tyrean Martinson

HOMESCHOOL

My oldest perches on her chair
her hand sifting through her hair,
her legs bent in frog pose.

My youngest daughter
pokes her lip with her pencil
and asks a question.

Around the table we ponder
subtraction, division and
that white cloud streaks   across   the   sky.

Concentration renewed,
scratching pencils do the work
of erasers, never used.

The white cloud streaks   across   the   sky
behind layers of   stretching   tree   branches
that call us to finish, to move on
                and   upward.

PUMPKIN PATCH

Muddy pools lead us
through the corn maze to giant
pumpkins, wheelbarrows
and slingshot contests that
we actually win this year.

So we bring home our prize,
golden and round, barely
squeezing
in the back of our van with
its smaller cousins.

There are plans for
the carving, and plans
for the painting,
but I just
want the seeds,
toasted crisp and
salted sweet.

Tyrean Martinson

NIGHT TERRORS
(Previously published at Every Day Poets)

Teeth clenched, fists knuckled,
he spasms awake, screaming
for a breath of air.
His dream enemies
dress in white, nurse's uniforms
or in the habits of nuns.
They are armed with
needles, stool softeners, bed
pans and extra pillows.
Three years in a charity
hospital gave him a mental scar,
after taking his leg.

RUNNING IN THE RHYTHM OF THE DARK

She finds four walls invasive
reminders of harsh words,
hard fists, and the ragged sobs
of her mother
so she runs into the darkness
running circles around the
church

She stops
by the bell tower, looks
up at the shadowy corners
where the bell waits
to ring away the cobwebs.
It stands still and she cannot,
running into night

She knows that boogiemen
don't lurk in dark corners,
but lie their way through the day,
keeping their deeds hidden with
false smiles, or false tears
as needed.

They aren't strangers
but the men we know
and call father, uncle, brother,
family friend
and yet, she knows some
are good, some are worthy

Tyrean Martinson

of trust.

She wonders why her father
who used to make her laugh
has turned out this way.
Is the pain from the hurt
or from the love she still
feels for the man he was
once upon a time?

Now
in a moment of quiet
when she is tired enough
to stand still again,
she tells me her favorite
book of the Bible
is Job.

THE HORSE IN THE WELL

My favorite bed time stories were from my Grandma Pearl, and her storytelling created a love of stories for me. When asked to write this story, I realized that the glory of sunset memories of my grandmother made it hard for me to capture the story inside the story. Her real life stories were hers, and as I tried to recall the details I felt like they were slipping away. My first draft awkwardly tripped over the paper. I couldn't seem to do the story just right, not like my grandmother used to tell. So I attempted to use her voice, and make it mine for a short while. I'm not sure I found it, but here is the story of "The Horse in the Well," originally told to me by Pearl Leta Paine Schneider.

Once upon a time when I was a little girl, I lived on a farm in Canada, just over the Washington border with my father, my mother, my two brothers, and my three sisters. I didn't go to school at the time because of my cleft palate. I hadn't had my surgery yet, and the opening in my mouth gave my mother a lot of trouble just to help me eat at home. I couldn't really talk properly so I was quiet most of the time. My brother Clayton and my sister Edna always seem to understand me anyway, and the horses spoke a language that I could understand with broad gestures that swept through their bodies. They were always good company even when I just stood on the lowest fence rail and watched them in the pasture.

One day my sister Edna and I stood together leaning against the fence watching the newest colt take springy steps away from his mother. We both wanted to touch his soft new fur, and stand by his side, but we weren't allowed inside the pasture without our brother Clayton. The mare might think we were a threat to her baby, and even when we leaned against the fence the first few days after his birth, she stamped at us to make sure we understood we weren't to come near.

This particular day we watched him, he was about a week old, and beginning to get a little adventurous, getting further and further from his mother in little short ambles. After a little distance, he would sprint back to her side, and kick his feet, proud of his little adventure.

In the corner of the pasture, an old well was covered up by a rounded set of boards. It hadn't been used in years, and the water was low in it. Even boarded up, I knew that I wasn't allowed to play by it. It really was just a long hole in the ground, with a board over the top that stood even with the grass. The horses even stayed away from it, although I don't know how they knew. They just did in the way that horses know things. But the colt didn't know yet.

As he explored the pasture, getting a little farther away from his mother all the time, he came closer and closer to that old well. Edna and I weren't really thinking about it, just watching him play and explore. He started to gallop back and forth, all over the pasture and to his mother. His lively enthusiasm was infectious and my sister and I smiled to see him run. But then he ran towards the end of the pasture where the old well was hidden in the grass, and he stumbled.

We heard the boards break, and then he squealed in terror and fell from our sight.

Edna wanted to go to him, but I held her back.

The mare screamed and pounded down to that end of the pasture. She looked down into the well, and screamed again, throwing her head in the air. Her eyes went white and wide, and she started to run in circles around that old well, unable to help her baby.

My brother Clayton came out of the barn and Edna shouted to him, "The colt's in the well, Clayton, the colt!"

He didn't say a word, but ran back into the barn. He came back with rope, and quickly tied it to the fence post closest to the well. He leaped over the fence in one motion, and then approached the mare, speaking quietly to her.

She reared at him, and then came down and stopped, looking at him with one wild eye.

He kept speaking, and she let him pass to the well. Then he climbed down into it, clinging to the rope.

I was so frightened, for the colt and for my brother, that I felt like I couldn't breathe. The air seemed suddenly thick with stillness, and the mare began to run back and forth, not crossing the rope, but still keeping vigil on the well. My sister and I clung to the fence, pressed up against it and gripping it hard, as if our grip could somehow help.

After what seemed to be too long, my brother's hand came up over the edge of the well. He carried the colt over his shoulders, and the colt lay there quietly as my brother came over the edge of the well, and crawled into the grass.

The mare stopped still, and watched until the colt tumbled off my brother's shoulders, and took shaking steps towards her. She bent and sniffed him all over, and he leaned against her.

My brother lay panting in the grass for a few minutes, and then he stood, and the mare whuffed his hair, and nuzzled his shoulder. He held her for a moment, and then he came to my sister and me. He swung us up in his arms, and held us close. I breathed in his work clothes smell, and the smell of the colt, and I knew things were all right again.

Light Reflections

Tyrean Martinson

haiku - shade

shade-dappled roadway
winding through trees –
    open horizons

WATERFALL

standing on my deck
 with my eyes closed, I can
 almost imagine

I'm standing
in the midst of
 a waterfall

the sound of rain on leaves all
around is almost the same.

Tyrean Martinson

TWOS IN THE MORNING

Two seasons intertwine
Two deer watch - ears up
Two huge pumpkins
Two walkers on a winding road
Two twittering birds

One turnaround
One truck
One lone jogger
One me on a bicycle

Another truck

Two pots of flowers
Two mailboxes
Two dogs at the door
Two daughters sleeping
My husband smiling

SO COLD
(Previously published at Every Day Poets)

even with heat
blasting on my face
I feel chilled
is winter within?

Tyrean Martinson

BREAKING THE STILLNESS
(Previously published at Every Day Poets)

silver blurring edges of poplar
trees reaching in muted light,
 brisk cold on my face,
foggy breath of my dogs and I,
 muffled train lowing,
 skimming car driving through slush:
 all these break the stillness
of a wet, winter morning.

sun rises, burning
through white clouds
softening the horizon,
blue sky cold freezes
dampness into ice
slipping back home,
I feel awakened, hardened, resolved
like trees that stand firm
through winter's chill.

JOSEPH'S DREAM

Dreaming deep of white angels in his sleep
Joseph envisions leaving her alone
Quietly put away without a peep
of impropriety, no throwing of stones
One Angel interrupts his dream to say
Fear Not, the child is the son of the Lord
Keep Mary safe as your wife on this day
You will raise His son, the Savior of the World
Joseph agrees, and wakes, his purpose clear
He will care for Mary, and hold her dear.

Tyrean Martinson

THE LIVING NATIVITY

"I was the littlest shepherd," he said,
Shining with love from toes to head.

"Oh," I said, "I didn't know it was you,
The littlest one in grey and blue."

"When the angels spoke, we knelt down,
Before journeying on to Bethlehem town."

"Yes, yes," I said, "I saw that. You were wonderful."
Then we stood in silence, with our hearts full.

A community coming together to recognize the birth,
Of our Savior Christ the Lord who brings us joy on earth.

CHRISTMAS LIGHTS SHIMMER INSIDE

Christmas lights shimmer on the bay
As we come home, warm inside
On a cold winter night
With Christ's birth in sight

His mother cradled him in the hay
We touched the donkey's hide
As we witnessed the living nativity
In scents, sounds, and bustling activity.

Christmas lights shimmer inside
As we come home, warm in our hearts
With Christ's birth in sight
In spite of the cold winter night.

Tyrean Martinson

SNOW FLURRIES

Sight of snow flurries
through the thick glass causes me
to step outside
into the cold swirling wind
to catch flakes on my tongue
and let the air sweep my soul
up
while my feet stay grounded
in the squeaky crunch of white

A SPRAY OF POWDER

Crunching snow under
stiff boots, crisp air against
my face, music pumped
through speakers,
the smell of fresh ski wax,
and I am finally there.
The climb from the parking lot
has warmed me up, and I'm
ready for the downhill, for
the ride full of moguls
and muscle strain, my two
young daughters and my
husband laughing with me
all the way down the mountain.

As we strap on skis and boards,
step into the chair lift line,
I overhear someone make a snide
remark about parents taking
their kids on black diamonds before
they're ready, and my daughters
and I smile at each other. My husband
laughs. At the top of the run, we wait
for a moment or two, and then we ski
and board away fast, leaving behind
a spray of powder.

Tyrean Martinson

BLACK DIAMONDS
(Previously published at Every Day Poets)

My black diamond daughters
love blue sky snow days,
skimming edges leaving behind
sprays of powder, and
a trail of laughter.

IN THE POWDER

Swiftly we drive to the snow that is fresh
Playing in powder is by far the best
We love the black mountains covered in white
Trees covered in crystals glittering bright
Skis, poles, snowboards, boots, bindings all packed
Extra gloves, warm clothes, waterproof jackets wrapped
Around us, with just our noses burning cold
We're ready for a fun day to unfold
First we climb from car to lodge to the lift
Our feet dangling high above the snow drift
Finally, we slide, turn, ride, spin, jump, skim
From late morning bright to dark skies that dim
Until muscles ache, gloves are damp, breath white
We drive home, heater on, under starry night.

Tyrean Martinson

SNOW CRUNCHING WALK

snow crunching walk by
moonlight, staring up at branches
dancing overhead in gusts
and the white covering the mulch
of leaves and brambles,
my dogs bound with ears flying
and I leap after them, renewed
by wonder, starlight, the deep bite
of cold on my cheeks and a thought
of God's love made manifest in
this moment, and long ago
in a stable, and all the moments
when we share His joy

PRAISE

So great my mind can't hold you or conceive
Of your vast, amazing, grace-filled being
It takes my soul a moment to believe
To surrender my notions of knowing
To the great I Am, the One who is three
Singing the Word in perfect harmony.
Created, directed, redeemed by love
That lights our ways like the wings of a dove
Whose feathers shimmer in the morning rays,
Shining for the truth, the life and the way.

Tyrean Martinson

SLUMBER PARTY SURPRISE

Ready for sleep,
Prepared to tell the slumber
Party girls to sleep,
I find them
Talking books
So I listen instead.

WE DANCE

We dance in taps, sneakers, foot undies, point shoes.
We dance to fast music, hip hop, and slow.
We want to get on with the beat, the show.

We may be only five, or sweet ninety-six,
we dance with heart, with rhythmic feeling
the music flow from toes to ceiling.

We stomp, tip tap, get down, and leap.
Across the room, we float, we jive, we scuff.
Don't you dare call what we do just fluff!

(For all the dancers I know)

Tyrean Martinson

CLEAN ENOUGH

My home teeters between
A comfortable mess and a mess
that makes me want to scream.
Sometimes more is less,
and sometimes less is more.

How can I even the score?
Shall I throw out the flowers that sit on the table?
Shall I vacuum the floor?
What tasks shall make me more comfortable?
What tasks will make me feel too bare?

An overly clean house feels like a dare,
as if I am floating in the emptiness of space.
Or stuck on a never ending, winding stair.
But if everything had an order and in its own place;
I could find a few missing things.

I guess it's decided then, I will pick up the strings
That the cat left after her favorite game,
and all of my daughters' favorite bling.
I will send the recycled paper into the flames,
vacuum the dirt from the floor.

Then my house will be clean enough.

The flowers are still bright, and can stay.

Light Reflections

ABOUT THE AUTHOR

Tyrean Martinson worships Jesus and loves her family in Washington State. She writes anywhere, and any time. You can find her online at Tyrean's Writing Spot, at twitter, and on Facebook.

Other books by Tyrean Martinson can be found at most online retailers.

If you like Tyrean's books, please give them a review at Goodreads.com, or at online retail sites.
Thank you.

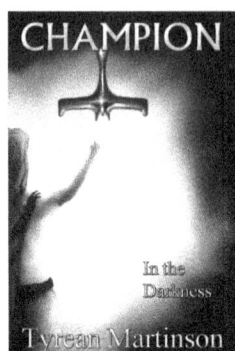

Clara's ready to become a master swordswoman. When she goes to meet with longtime mentor Dantor, Clara is told she's destined to become the Champion, a fabled hero who arises in a time of struggle. Despite her doubts, Clara must find a way to become the Champion her people need.

Whether Clara is ready or not, the evil Kalidess has wormed her way into Septily's court.

Clara is aided by another mentor, Stelia, whose knowledge of their enemy is both a bane and a blessing. As evil threatens their land, Clara and Stelia must find the strength to overcome the darkness.

What Readers Are Saying:

"Excellent writing and strong Christian faith meet in this adventure for young readers. This is a great book for young and old alike." Denise P. at Amazon.

"Champion in the Darkness is YA fantasy/Christian fiction, and while the religious side was evident, it never overwhelmed the story" By A. McCall at Amazon.

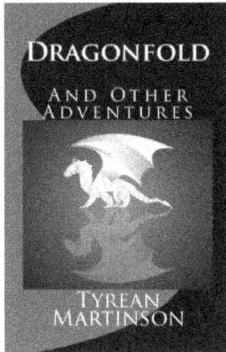

Azami has a gift with origami. Will she master it in time to save herself from bondage? Find out in "Dragonfold."

Joanne lost more than her honor in the war, she lost her will to live. When bandits attack her homestead, will she stand or fall in "Enough to Do?"

And just who is Captain Wrath under that itchy, false wig? Find out more in "The Identity of Captain Wrath."

Dragonfold and Other Adventures includes imaginative stories and poems, written between 2008 and 2013 by Tyrean Martinson. Some of these adventures have been previously published, and others are waiting to be discovered for the first time.

www.ingramcontent.com/pod-product-compliance
Lightning Source LLC
Chambersburg PA
CBHW020518030426
42337CB00011B/447